Thanks and that

First and foremost I'd like to thank every si... ...the people who were kind enough to pick me up and give me a lift. I ... ...of all your names as most of you if not all of you will never get t... ...the fact I decided ... ...next I'd like to thank everyone I met along the way and anyone involved for making it easily the best 8 days of my life to date.

Special Strangers

The Hitcher at Maidstone: I'd forgotten your name after about 10 minutes of you telling me it the 2nd time but you have a note of mine and hopefully you can find me on facebook and get to read this thanks for the smoke and company.

The Iraqi man: Thank you for giving me £20 to help me on my travels considering I returned with 2 Euro's left it definitely made a difference.

Frankie the Frenchie: About the 20th person I'd approached at Dover Ticket Station but the first person to agree to give me a lift to the continent. You were a brilliant help and I hope your dad is ok.

French Abertay Student: Your name also escapes me, hopefully my mad life allows me to find you again somehow. Thank you for stopping and picking up a strange boy at the side of a random back road.

French School Teacher: Thank you for the lift, the beer and the bag.

François: Thank you for squeezing me into your people carrier with all your luggage and family and giving me a lift across Italy, I could never have made it so successfully if it hadn't been for you.

Verona Policeman: Thank you for giving me directions and helping out an ignorant Brit with no Italian.

The Italian Man in the Train Station: Thank you for keeping me company and helping me figure out Verona Train Station

The Italian Woman in the Train Station: Thank you for helping me with the ticket machine. I might have missed the train without you.

The Elderly German Couple: Thanks for the German Atlas it made the rest of the trip home so much easier.

Biller Der Jäger: Thank you for the opticians trip, they now stay on my face a lot easier.

Hermen: Thank you for being such a jolly German

Turk: Thank you for giving me such a hugely helpful lift and the German lesson

Hungarian Family: Thanks you so very much for everything you did for me, the lift, the food, and making me feel so welcome.

Robbie: Thanks for the lift and all of the wonderful conversation you were definitely the most interesting companion.

Helpful Organizations

Team Susan: Good Dan Still Not Done It, Campbell Camp Bro Simple Simpson, Cameron Wiz Kalifa Reid (and Susan Herself the tough old bird) thank you so much for dragging me around with you and also knowing absolutely no Italian.

X-Rafting: Thanks for being so helpful and letting us use your site to get the boat fixed.

Loughborough Uni Boaters: Thanks for the loan of the stove, the company and putting up with my travel exacerbated madness.

Feel Free: Thank you for the loan of the BA, my other option was to duct tape an airbag to myself. (if you don't believe me then wait till you hear what my helmet was).

Home team support

Mum: thanks for not attempting to talk me out of it and supporting me you really should stop worrying about me though.

Dave: Holding down the fort while I was out dragging myself about Europe and having a fully stocked fridge/freezer for me to return to.

Readers: Thanks for passing this on ;P

Contents

The numbers in brackets after section titles indicate a relevance to one of the sections in the final section Pen Chewing Reflections

Day By Day

Through Britain I've always gone with the good old thumb hitch, standing at service station exits and motor way on ramps. This trip was no different, on my first day I managed to travel the majority of Britain ending up at a Maidstone services where I met another hitcher and spent the night. I didn't have a real plan for my route down and just took lifts off anyone who stopped and in lots of little dribs and drabs I made it most of the way to Dover.

The morning of the 2nd day took me forever to reach Dover as not much Dover bound traffic stops at services so close by and the South East of England are quite unsympathetic to hitchhikers in comparison to the rest of Britain. The whole way through England I was being passed by drivers heading in groups to the Du Mann's rally. Unfortunately my lift to Dover was just passing through and not going to the continent so hanging around outside the terminal I was asking drivers for lifts and eventually caught Frankie who along with a couple of French Women got me to a services North of Dijon.

On the 3rd Day, after sleeping through an alarm I set out as sun rose and got a lift as far as Lyon. From Lyon I spent a long time flitting between some smaller French towns to Chambéry(nearly giving up and getting a train). I then spent the next few hours hitching/walking myself round in a big circle. eventually being dropped off by a French school teacher at a Péage until a Romanian trucker took me over the border to Italy. From the Services there I got a lift from a kind French family all the way to Verona which was about 65km south of Where Campbell, Dan and Camo were.

Saturday morning (the small hours) found me snaking my way along train tracks heading for the station and eventually finding my way and camping out on the platform till I could get a train North and hitch the last 14km West to the town where the boys had camped for the night. I woke them up, we packed up the car and headed for the Noce region for some kayaking and camping next to a rafting centre and had a wee tipple.

On Sunday the valley we'd camped in had some bike race running through it so we headed for Austria and found a wee campsite where we met some boaters from Loughborough Uni and Me and Campbell got gibbled and chatted pish till god knows what hour of the morning.

The Monday I got some boating in with the boys and the boaters from Loughborough. having hitched I didn't have any kit but between spare kit from Dan, and Campbell a BA from Feel Free Rafting and a watermelon I got on and down the Imst gorge and it all went swimmingly. To clarify to any kayakers reading this I mean swimmingly in the good way. The others went on to do another river while I hung out with Derek at the get out and we went back to the campsite for dinner and a few drinks.

6

Tuesday we got up and went for breakfast I packed up as much as my stuff as I could find in Susan and then ran away hitching myself back to Glasgow about half 11, 12 oclock. A few lifts up into Germany and I was in awe at the approachability and generosity of German drivers on the autobahn. After trying for a while my conventional hitchhiking method I began to approach drivers and ask them directly. Nice cars too. By mid-afternoon I was in a lift from services outside Nürnberg to Köln. Eventually getting tuckered out and camping up on a bench for the night.

A couple hours into Wednesday sleeping was difficult and I got up and started asking folk for lifts again. I spotted a car with a GB number plate and asking the driver, who to my surprise was a Hungarian woman, got myself a lift all the way to a Manchester services, via Nottingham, with her and her family. Then my final lift, essentially to my door from a Paisley man named Robert Robertson I got after attempting to thumb it from the exit road, getting bored and walking around asking drivers for a lift.

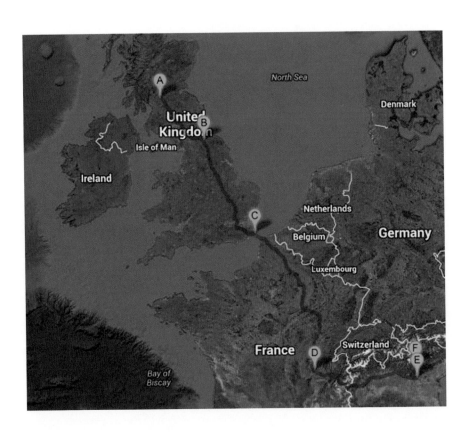

Down t' Road

Getting Going (1)

Bored and unsatisfied with my summer travels so far I decided I'd go and visit some friends of mine in the Alps. Rejecting a job offer and £60 spare in the bank hitchhiking was really the only thing for it. 8 days travelling, 5 European countries, some really interesting people and some really interesting experiences later I had an amazing time.

To fully explain the situation, I was less than a fortnight back from a surf trip in France to sort out some finance issues. This had put a spanner in the works for my original plans to hitch from the West Coast where I was surfing to the South East of France where some friends of mine were kayaking in Bréançon. My only plan in the near future was that I had my Grad Ball on the 28th in Glasgow so I needed to be home for that.

After looking at my options I decided that the earliest I could leave for this would be the 15th of June. After some arm twisting from friends to do things here in Glasgow, coupled with my own anxieties about the feasibility of it all I eventually managed to throw myself out the door on the morning of the 17th. I sent Campbell a Facebook message telling him I was on my way and jumped on a train to Uddingston then walked to the services with a sign tied to my bag saying "DOVER FRANCE ITALY". Expectedly I made it to the services before anyone stopped to pick me up.

The Hitch

Standing at the exit road from the services I stuck my thumb out and got hitching. A short while later a couple stopped and took me as far as the services at Gretna, from there I got a lift with a guy in his 30s who showed me an album of photo's on his Ipad of a factory we passed on the way. From the services he dropped me at I was picked up by an ex-army serviceman who took me to Scotch Corner, probably not the fastest route but it meant I didn't need to tackle the cluster of random Motorways around Manchester and got myself down the M1 to a services near Cambridge from a Girl from the area and her boyfriend who's from Glasgow and the 2 of them go to Uni in Aberdeen I think (this was before I'd started taking notes).

From Cambridge I was picked up in a van by a man who takes leftover/overflow from M&S supply lorries down to the Maidstone Services. As I arrived at the services I started out hitching by the on ramp from the roundabout onto the Motorway but after a while I began to think the spot wasn't great so decided to go see if there was a better one up next to the services, on arriving there I met a fellow hitcher who's name has completely escaped me, I should have written it down. He has mine so hopefully he will find me on facebook.

After this I walked about asking some drivers, tried to hitch from various points around the services and the roundabout and then as I was about to head back to the roundabout it was pushing 11 o'clock and I walked past, lets call him Preston since I'm pretty sure that's where he went to Uni, I walked past Preston and he said "Hey, it's getting late, if you want to call it a night I have a joint we can share." I turned, swayed a little then gave in and said yeah alright, he tried another 5 or 10 mins of hitching before we grabbed some cardboard from the recycling, made ourselves some beds, camped out under a tree next to the services, set some tunes playing and had a smoke.

He had grown up in Dubai and Went to Uni in England, as I said I think Preston. Now that sounds like an incredibly similar situation to David, whom I'd met while on the surf trip less than 2 weeks before who'd gone to Sheffield Uni, so I asked him if he knew him and turns out they went to school together. Now at this point in writing this story I have discovered a photo of Preston on the UCLAN Canoe Club page and have sent them a message to try and get his real name.

A slow Starting Thursday

We woke up about 6ish and started packing up all our stuff, or well Preston did, I lay there with a bit of stoneover for an extra 10 mins and then dragged myself up and started packing to be finished before him and leave my name on a pad of paper for him to find me. I walked down to the roundabout to hitch, leaving him to his original spot and not long later saw him tear past me in an orange ford focus. So I went up and started to hitch from his spot and got a lift within half an hour.

Lifts on Thursday morning were terrible apart from the kind Iraqi man and his workmates who picked me up and gave me 20 quid for my travels. It took me several hours to make it to Dover which is normally 40-45 min drive from where I started. My lift to Dover was unfortunately not going to France either but just passing through Dover. I spent the following hour or so charging my phone and talking to drivers about the ticket office/car park if they would have space for another traveller[1].

I had asked the desk how much a ticket on foot would be and was just about ready to give up and pay my way over the channel, but the prospect of spending over a quarter of my budget for the whole trip was enough for me to go and walk around 1 last time. I am so glad I did. Had I not I would never have met Frankie, a kind French man who had being living and was married in the UK. As I walked out the terminal to do one last lap of the car park I got about 10-15 steps out the building and this large man wanders out from behind a corner and looked a little intimidating but I figured I would ask anyway. I had never been so relieved to hear the phrase "I don't see why

---

[1] For anyone who doesn't know, when you pay for a car on the ferry it includes up to 7 passengers and it's really simple to change your ticket to include an extra person.

not." Taking me over the channel on the Pride of Burgundy(Why P&O have this obsession with grand sounding names for their ships I do not know).

Frankie through France

Frankie was en route to visit his dad who had gone into hospital and was able to give me a lift all the way to somewhere between Reims and Dijon which is a fair chunk of my journey through France covered. The whole way down the French Motorways he would arbitrarily start tooting his horn and we spent a lot of time chatting about the weather. As we travelled through the North of France we went through some pretty heavy rain. The closer we got to where he was turning off the Motorway though, the better the weather got till there was even some blue in the sky when I got out the car.

Now route planning and stuff was easy in Britain with the small amount of data allowance I have on my mobile contract being enough for me to look through some maps and also for keeping in touch with people. But once on the continent the rules are different and you get some ridiculous charges . lucky for me Vodafone have a good deal where if you use your phone once you are charged and then have use of the phone for the entire day. The only problem is that before I left I didn't clarify what constitutes a day and who's days we go by, is it just the next 24 hours or does it reset at midnight and which midnight?

The Power of Passive Advertisement

I walked around the services asking folk about lifts and found an Irishman who dangled the prospect of a lift all the way to Italy in front of me but snatched it away by following up his original story with the fact his car had broken down and he was no longer going to Italy, he said after some food and stuff he could give me a lift a little further down the motorway though. While sitting about in the services with my sign, "VALSESSIA ITALY", propped up on the table and trying to use some wifi, I was spoken to by a couple of French women.

They were travelling in my direction much further than the Irish man and were kind enough to offer me a lift to a services just North of Dijon and after they'd had a cigarette they set off with me in the back seat. One of them spoke little English while the other was fluent, although she did occasionally struggle with my speedy Scottish accent. So we managed to chat about some pretty interesting topics, rent prices around Scotland, the nature of British folk, my degree and what my academic plans were. The whole while this was going on one of the women was essentially having the conversations twice translating between myself and her travel buddy.

Dropping me off at the services about 10 or 11ish at night the 2 of them left me to fend for myself again and continued on. For the next few hours I wandered around, swapping between hitching from a roundabout exit and asking drivers, using my newly learned French phrase, "Je Vais On Italia", taught to me by my previous lift.

Eventually I got tired about 1am on Friday morning and decided to call it quits for the night.

I had spotted 3 lorries about the place with Italian number plates and decided I would catch a couple hours rest and then hopefully catch them leaving to ask for a lift, now knowing Campbell and Dan were in Valsessia, for the night at least. Finding some WIDDEN PALLETS!! Out the back of the services I nicked one for a mattress and dragged it into a bush for some cover from the prospect of rain.

Language Barrier I

Unfortunately I slept through my alarm and woke up about 4 in the morning, packed all my things up and replaced the pallet where I'd got it from. I even managed to squeeze in a shower in the services before setting off. I went to the roundabout and started hitching. As I stood there a pine tree in front of me in the centre of the roundabout had the top section illuminated by the sun while the rest was in the shadow of a services building sitting behind me. I shivered my way through the next half hour or so until the sun came up over the services and warmed me up a little.

Eventually a French man with very limited English picked me up and told me he could take me as far as Cannes in the south of France. At one point in the drive he was on the phone to a friend of his and they ended up doing a little bit of translation between me and my driver which helped somewhat.

Changing the route

As I checked things out I realised that I would be faster to Milan if I went East at Lyon so managed to communicate this to the guy and he agreed to drop me off as the motorway ran basically through the city centre. There were also trains and busses from Lyon and Milan where Campbell and Dan were spending their Friday before grabbing Camo from the Airport and heading North East to camp for the night.

The man missed the turn offs though and ended up dropping me at the bottom of an off ramp in the hard shoulder and I walked over a bridge to go in the other direction. Eventually I realised how useless this spot was for hitching and decided to walk the 4km up a back road running parallel to the main road to Lyon, all the while holding up my newly created "MILANO" sign to my side on the off chance I caught a local heading to Italy. I didn't and instead was picked up by a French Student who was about 19 and is heading to Abertay University next year to do Bioscience. While thanking him profusely for stopping he responded with "I would have wanted someone to stop if I was you" which reinstalled my confidence in the French and probably what stopped me going for the bus there and then (well that coupled again with the price of transport). He gave me a lift to the turn off for a little suburb of Lyon which was also an awful spot for hitching next to what was essentially the border of a dual carriageway upgrading itself to a motorway.

Getting out of Lyon

After a few minutes of hitching I moved to a hard shoulder of an on ramp to the motorway a little further along and tried to hitch for a bit before realising the traffic was too fast and heavy for someone to stop easily and clambered down into the suburb and walked my way along to another motorway slip road, again standing in the hard shoulder before also giving up on that spot.

I decided that I would walk myself up the motorway until I found a better spot or a services to hitch from, standing around wasn't doing me any favours and at least this way I was getting closer to catching up with Team Susan. I eventually found another motorway entrance where the cars would drive up to a traffic island and stop before turning left onto the motorway. Here I returned a phone call which turned out to be from FDM and the woman I spoke to wasn't sure why I'd received a call so sent an email upstairs and I left it at that.

Language Barrier II

A couple of French women stopped a short time later and took me in the back of their car while heading for Grenoble. During the ride we confused one another and they thought I wanted to be dropped off at the nearest train station and so they did in St Quentin. I figured here I would just hop on a train to Chambéry and hitch from there but at the last minute for some reason changed my mind and decided to head back to Lyon and get a bus which was 35 Euro, about the same as a foot ticket on the ferry. Changed my ticket and got 5 Euro's or so in refund from the helpful woman behind the ticket counter who was in awe at my mission.

At this point my will power, due to a combination of sleep deprivation and some bad luck was running low. Then I was using the internet on my phone to figure out times and prices of travel to Milan I realised that there was only 1 bus a day and that the train would cost me extortionate amounts and also ran infrequently so it was unlikely I'd get one destined for Milan before Dan and Campbell decided to leave or for a decent price. It was here that I remembered myself

No Cost Comes at a Price

I wish during this point of the journey that someone could have been there narrating the journey and my own internal monologue, in absence of this I think I went a bit mental for a bit and started doing it myself. I left the station mutter inspiring things to myself and headed back up to the motorway to again start hitching towards Italy. I eventually got a lift toward Chambéry but got dropped again in the hard shoulder, this time just arbitrarily at the side of a motorway, so I could clamber about and get myself to a slip road onto the other motorway in the direction I wanted to go.

Climbing up the side of a bridge and walking over a hill through a field I began to wonder what animal was kept in a field, naturally my mind jumped to the worst conclusion of a raging bull but I was able to ignore that and stay optimistic that it was some sheep or at the very least that the Bull was up wind. As I got over the peak of the hill there were some cows but they were fenced off and I was in a field occupied by horses, stopping to feed them some grass and having them follow me down the path a bit toward the farm house(which I was worried a French Farmer might appear out of until I saw a car drive off down the track and allowed myself to assume that meant he was out) The horses got bored and I climbed through a barbed wire fence, doing some gymnastics to avoid the barbs and a wire which I had to assume was electrified to be on the safe side.

I then followed down the path which went under the motorway alongside a train track and turned off in the wrong direction. With this side of the motorway underpass not scalable to reach the motorway, at least not without enduring some severe nettle stings, I made a very quick decision to hop over the train tracks and climb up the other side and onto the slip road between the motorway I'd been dropped off on and the one I wanted to be travelling along.

Chambéry

I was then picked up by some French women (they did seem to take pity on me the French women) . I was dropped off once again at a random point at the side of the motorway close to a crossover with another motorway I wanted to be on. Here I dropped down the side and into an industrial park near Chambéry. Emerging from the bushes growing along the side of the motorway I was confronted with a cardboard skip which I stole some sign material from, receiving a look from a Frenchman sitting in a car. I'm still not sure of it's meaning, I think a mix of disbelief and disgust at what he'd just witnessed.

Here I then trekked through into the city and up to the motorway on ramp, this involved clambering through some forest and I ended up with some cuts bruises and an inordinate amount of nettle stings to the point where I felt I'd developed an immunity to them. Also watching a small lizard run away from me up a drainage duct which was reminiscent of a Crash Bandicoot chase level where you would run from an enemy on the back of an animal and hop about the different levels. Eventually habituation kicked in or the play dead reflex and it stopped as I passed it by.

I was then given a lift to a services just passed Chambéry where I walked around asking truckers for lifts as well as other people until I got tired of rejection and went to the exit road for the motorway and stood hitching until I got a lift from a woman in a hippy van. This was another unfortunate lift of 3 where I was once again dumped at the side of the motorway at a point where 2 motorways crossed, a lot of that going on between Lyon and Italy it seems. I climbed up a concrete slope about ¾ of a meter wide, assisted by a fence and crossed the road and climbed down a similar slope on the other side. Here I wandered down into the ditch to get away from the motorway traffic a bit.

14

KB'd by the motorway bouncers and determined madness (2)

Some workers of l'autoroute stopped in the hard shoulder and signalled to me to climb the fence into a field which in most circumstances I was happy to do but in this case the field contained a farmer ploughing or something so didn't want to stop dealing with them to then have to deal with him. After some attempts at communicating between myself and these Frenchmen who spoke no English they took me about 500m along the road and put me through a gate in the fence(something it still baffles me why they didn't just do in the first place). I then began trekking 6km towards a Rest Area.

In France you get a variety of Rest Stops ranging from big service stations similar to the popular ones on British Motorways down to smaller ones which are just a toilet and a play park in a little wooded car park just off the motorway. This rest stop was one of the latter and would receive very little traffic so at this point my plan had become (given it was about 8oclock and the road was slightly quieter) to hide at the side of the motorway in the bushes until a break in the traffic allowed me to get to the central reservation. Hopefully I wouldn't have to wait too long and a similar break then allowed me over to the other side as this was where I needed to be to get back to the motorway I wanted to.

Luckily this plan never needed to happen as I found a river which ran beneath the motorway which I was able to cross and begin trekking the 6km's back to the motorway I wanted to hitch along. As I wandered up a path I stumbled across I noticed a river flowing next to me, not just a small stream but a motorway sized torrent of Alpine water flowing south. As I got closer I realised there was a bridge across the river as part of the motorway I wanted to be on.

So far on this trip I had picked up on the fact that the bridges of the motorways had no hard shoulders so I began to panic and my brain started coming up with all sorts of wild theories on how I would get myself across the river. These ranged from dangerous to mildly insane and included shimmying myself along the bridge overhanging the water. Again luckily my brain and its wild ideas were silenced when I happened upon a lake just South East of where the 2 motorways crossed.

There were people hanging about the lake and camping and stuff that I could see on the other side, on my side of the lake I came across a French Nudist sunbathing. Now most people I know would probably have avoided the whole situation but me being me and enjoying a bit of casual nudity I approached the man and struck up a chat with him which ended with me going skinny dipping in the lake and then afterwards having more conversation with the man and him offering me a lift to a better hitching spot back towards Chambéry. So I accepted and we got dressed and headed for his car at the other end of the lake.

Knowing that there are a lot of French nude beaches I asked him if it was one but he told me that it wasn't and he just likes to sunbathe there. I also found out that he was a local school teaher and sometimes takes his lunch breaks, depending on his class schedule by the lake to relax. Dropping me off at a Péage and telling me I could walk along the toll booths on a path, giving me a couple beers and new bag as the one I'd been carrying my sleeping bag in had burst and I was now carrying the other things in the bag wrapped up in my sleeping bag under my arm.

Now the man wasn't lying there was a path but as I walked along it I encountered a locked gate so had to skip out around it when a worker of the tolls came over to ask what I was doing, so I explained the situation, in a little more sheepish way than the reality so as to instill some sympathy and she took me down into some underground tunnels which I assume run under all these toll stations as emergency exits.

Finn-It-aly

After getting to the other side of the tolls I walked up to the far end of a car park and began hitching again. At French Toll Stations there is a defined line where no road marking shall cross and the lanes of the motorway just vanish and chaos ensues until the other side of the tolls a few hundred meters and the motorway begins again. The spot I was hitching at was at the point where the motorway begins again or just 100m or so before that. After a short while a Romanian trucker called Colain pulled over for me and I had my lift into Italy and told me I had a lift to Milan, which I'd now decided I was going to use as my hitching end point and get trains the rest of the way to catch up with Susan and the boys.

Language Barrier III

As we drove to Italy I felt a mixture of relief and disbelief at my efforts, the Romanian spoke little English but we did manage to communicate to some extent. I slowly noticed as the country side turned from French farmlands to Alpine mountain ranges towering on either side of me. The Alps are fantastic. It's like Scottish Mountain ranges but stretched up thousands of meters, with little towns built all up and down the side of them. Throughout the Alps I have found there is a similar theme but each area has its own little subtleties in the towns. Huge waterfalls and massive rivers carve through the mountainsides and at one point I saw an Alp which from its peak to the foot transitioned through every different type of Scottish hill/mountain-side, from rocky peaks to brown / green grassy areas and hillside woodlands.

Not long after entering the Alps we began a massive climb up to the Fréjus Road Tunnel where the Italians still keep a border and had large booths where the lorry was scanned for heat signatures. This was by far the biggest Alpine Tunnel I'd been through burrowing through a 12.87km of Alpine Rock and having the Italian French border somewhere inside as well as its own radio station. As we got through the other side I started noticing the little differences in the towns mainly that they were built over more levels and contained more religious buildings/architecture than I'd noticed in France.

This is where language barrier 3 brought me back to the reality of my task. As the driver pulled over into a service station and informed me that due to his driving program he could no longer drive and would have to stop for the night and continue on to Milan in the morning at 9am. Unwilling to give up I got out and went down to the service station, by this point my phone had ran out of battery and I had no car charger and I'd forgotten to lift my European converters.

French Passage Through Italy

I attempted to hitch at the exit onto the motorway and was told off by some Italian motorway workers saying that you're not allowed to hitch at all and I must go and talk to people about the services. As my phone had died I first went into the services to see if they sold converters because I only had my UK plug and forgot my USB cable. They didn't so I just went out and began asking drivers where they were heading and if they had room. Asking a family of French people they told me that they had no room for me with all their luggage. After this I asked a few more people and found a coach that was headed for Milan that had pulled into the services. Speaking to one of the drivers who had little English he told me to wait for the other driver to speak with him about a lift. The other driver had no English or I was too tired to understand his accent but as I was chatting with him Francois, a member of the French family approached me and told me if I didn't mind being cramped they would be able to make some space for me.

This was brilliant, there was a people carrier and a car travelling with 4 adults and 6 kids to Croatia, so I got my stuff in the people carrier and ran back into the services to buy myself a USB cable so I could charge my phone. 19.99 Euro's was stupidly expensive but my phone was necessary for this leg as I needed to find out where Team Susan had set up camp for the night. Getting on the phone to them I found out they were stopping in a place called Arco at the north end of Lake Garda in North East Italy. Francois and the convoy were going close to an Italian city at the South end of lake Garda called Verona and this was about 60-70km away from Arco.

Sleeping most of the way after travelling through a thunderstorm and a mad traffic jam I was dropped off at an Italian Toll station at the exit for Verona Airport. This was about midnight in Italy and so it was dark and there are no pedestrian routes from these places to the main city as far as I could tell so I set off following the dual carriageways and motorway signs for Verona headed for the train station.

When travelling with the French family I accidentally sent a text to Camo after midnight on one of the days which I'd decided not to use my phone so as to not rack up too high a phone bill so that meant another £3. What was worse was that I didn't realise for ages so I refrained from using my phone for a long time until it occurred to me that I'd done so and by then there was only a few hours left in the day.

Verona After Dark

Now if you remember a while back I was talking about sunrise and a tree after sleeping through the Italian lorries leaving what you might not have realised is that from then till now was all the 3rd day of my travels. What an exhaustingly eventful day, I'd clambered over woodland, farmland hills and motorways, met the nudist teacher and gone skinny dipping, wandered slightly lost through some French towns, encountered a few language barriers and been given a lift across Northern Italy by a French family and that's a short version. The madness wasn't over yet though.

I thought I knew roughly where I was from using the remains of a map I'd got off the internet earlier, just what was still sitting in my phone's memory so I started walking towards the city and the road signs confirmed I was going roughly in the right direction. I ended up in a little suburb in the South West of Verona where I heard some shouting and cheering which turned out to be a late night each volleyball game in a flood lit pitch. Really tempted to go and join them I resisted and continued on cause I really wanted to get to the train station and this close to the end I was eager to catch team Susan.

Further wandering over roads and fields brought me walking through what I think was an out of season vineyard and then seeing some structures, headed towards them cause I figured there would be a much easier road to follow into the city centre. Approaching the Building's I realised they were houses, big houses. The family dog began barking it's head off at me and I panicked. I had no idea if this dog was in the field with me, or if the gate was open for me to run out on to the road if I had to try escape it, if the owner was in, if Italians kept guns. All I knew was that it was about 1am a dog was angry and I'd imagine the owner wouldn't be too pleased in this situation either.

Approaching the station (3)

Turns out all was well the dog was fenced off and the gate was open and once I got far enough away I think the dog stopped barking, either that or I got out of earshot. I managed to follow this road past some early morning bin men or something who I showed my sketchy map to and they gave me some sort of directions but didn't speak English so I didn't really get it. I continued snaking along the train tracks which I sort of understood the direction of heading to the train station all converging from different destinations from outside the city.

I took another wrong turn and realised as I started to walk out of Verona and into the wilderness again. Turning round I noticed an Italian police car driving towards me and flagged them down and was able to get directions to the train station off them. They suggested I get a taxi but I refused and got walking. As I walked through the town(not knowing the train times) I was assessing trees and sleep spots in case I had a few hours to crash before a train. Getting to the station other people had done the same there were couples and groups of people ass nestled up under tree's on this promenade outside the station, clearly finding the local hotels and such too expensive. I got into the station about 3am and saw there were some trains leaving in a couple hours. I managed to work out That the train I wanted was the one headed for Bregenz getting off at Roveretto. As I sat trying to work out if I had made the right call I was approached by an Italian man who spoke little English asking for a cigarette, I did not have one.

We then spent the next hour or so trying to communicate, he managed to reassure me about how to get my ticket tell me that I could get a discount if I waited for the station ticket machines to open rather than paying on the train and communicate through writing on my pad of paper and in some broken English. Sitting in a shelter on the platform he went for a 5 min nap, I followed about 15 mins later leaving him a note and I woke up to a back-up alarm I set myself half an hour before my train left.

Arriving at Milo

The man was still asleep at the other end of the shelter. I thought about leaving him another note but didn't have the time or the brain power to come up with anything to say. Also looking back he probably wouldn't be able to read it anyway. As I stood at the ticket machine, I'd managed to get through to booking my ticket and then I stood there and tried to work out where to put my money in, an Italian woman barged in front of me saying "no!" She grabbed the money from my hand, pushed some more buttons on the screen and then placed the money into the machine and then shoved my ticket and my change into my hand and walked off. She wasn't even waiting to use it.

Running back up the stairs with minutes to spare I punched my ticket(some European thing I still don't fully understand) and jumped on the train. On the train I got some more help from a father of a family to confirm I was on the right train and what stop to get off at. Then we arrived at Milla. I remembered from looking at a map that Milla was closer to Arco than Roveretto so, with the protest of the father, I got off and started walking what I thought was the direction of Arco. Coming to the first bus stop I saw there was a bus in half an hour going to Arco and this is when it started to hit home that I'd made it.

Having half an hour I figured I might as well try and get the last little bit for free, following the bus route, mainly I might have taken a wrong turn, I walked along the roadside hitching until I got to a bus stop at the edge of Milla heading out onto the main road to Arco. Standing hitching from here outside a little set of shops which were starting to open a man stopped 3 mins before the bus arrived and gave me a lift to Arco, dropping me off at the foot of the road to the campsite. Here I began getting unreasonably happy but was too knackered from the travels to express it in any way.

Campeggio

Walking up the road I reached the campsite and wandered in for a look for Susan. I got round the whole site and couldn't see any sign of them. I wondered if I'd just missed the old girl and was about to walk round again when I realised that there was a sign saying there was another camp site 800m up the road, so I got marching with a huge cheeser on my face, still slightly worried that I might not be able to find them. I had no idea where there were, all I had was Arco. As I rounded the corner expecting to see the entrance way to the next campsite I was greeted by an even more wonderful sight. Susan the sexy beast parked up in a layby boats strewn around the side and a tent accompanied by a hammock everything I'd been dreaming of for the past 3 days.

Joining the Ranks of Team Susan

Wake Up Call

Walking up to the hammock I peered over to double check it was in fact Campbell. After a couple seconds debating with myself(his shitey little wispy beard threw me off) I leant down kissed him on the cheek and he roused, looking up from the hammock as I yelled, "I made it!". After some morning groans and a stretch he shouted into the tent "Hey guys, remember when I said I was going to wake up to a face hanging over me... It happened." A voice from the tent I recognised as Dan replied, surprised, "Oh is Glenn here."

The boys got up. Campbell, his usual useless morning self, watched Dan pack up the car; Dan, somehow swapped nationalities, now appeared Iranian; and Camo, well he was just being Camo. They all packed up their stuff, I had my first shot of Alcool(95% alcohol they use to fortify wine on the continent), and rammed it all back in Susan. For those of you who haven't caught up yet; Susan is Dan's sorry excuse for a car; a wonder to behold but only because she still ran.

Travelling with the Lads

Soon after setting off something was up with the car, given this was somewhere between 8 and 10 am the morning I arrived and after being up most of the night roaming Verona and after the 3 days of travel in the sun and going slightly insane I don't really remember what went on for this portion of the day. We had to tighten a wheel and got lost in some wee Italian town for a while. Arriving in the Noce valley I was dropped with Susan and the keys. The boys went off down a river and I rambled about the local area in search of a camp spot accompanied by a 1.5L camelpak of cheap Italian Wine. Oh we'd also been to some shops and got food and 5L of Wine and a bottle of Alcool for getting gibbled.

On the way down the river Dan put a hole in his boat, riding around on the bonnet and roof of his car to pick It up and then driving to the get out we saw some other people out rafting and boating on the river, chatting to them they gave us the name of a company where we might get use of a heat gun to repair the split in the boat. For some reason the rest of team Susan decided that was a silly idea and we should go to a campsite and use plug sockets there to use the heat gun and repair the boat.

After driving for many kilometres and not getting anywhere with a campsite hunt they changed their minds and we went to X-Rafting in Caldes and they were more than helpful letting us use their power sockets and tools to get the boat back in working condition. We also realised while walking about the site that there was a campsite around this rafting centre so we decided just to pitch our tents and stay here for a few nights. Another night sleeping rough with Campbell's hammock and tarp above me and ground sheet beneath me these bunk beds are where we spent the night with Dan and Camo next to us in the tent.

"It goes something like this: you sit in a tree with a lot of alcohol and drink until you fall out of the tree in a drunken stupor."

After fixing up the boat and setting up camp we cooked ourselves a ratatoullie tank that the guys had bought before my arrival and dug in with some forks; One of which I'd pinched off the Pride of Burgundy to eat my pasta. Drinking began and eventually migrated into the tree where we had a guitar, booze and a merry old time, I think we also may have passed out in the tree for short periods of time; I definitely came to midway through the others singing a song. At some point in the proceedings Campbell and Camo went to bed and me and Dan decided to strip off and continue drinking; taking possuming to the next level, the naked possum. To us this was a hilarious idea up till a point where we realised it was night and cold and the tree bark was quite uncomfortable to the bare skin.

After my escapades through France and skinny dipping in the lake I had decided to make it a point to go skinny dipping in every country I stopped in. In the end I didn't manage this cause no one was up for it in the cold glacier melt of Italy and Austria but I managed a substitute, this was 2 out of the 3 countries I'd be staying in which some kind of comic nudity took place.

Once we realised the discomfort of being naked in the tree we clambered down to pick up our clothes and went to bed. Gibbled.

KB'd from Italy

In the morning I woke up underneath Campbell's hammock and found a small Italian man wandering around picking up litter. I got up and started to clean up some of our mess and then a short while later the other boys joined me just before some local authorities appeared and cleared everyone off the campsite as a bike race was taking place in the Noce valley that day. With the valley off limits we decided to make the journey into Austria the day early.

Campbell had admitted to me that he was worried he'd accidentally sent a text to his girlfriend from my phone after midnight which I'd decided was the crossover from one day to the next in the phone use deal. While I checked it out I noticed he hadn't and I handed it to him to read a reply, at this point he accidentally tapped a button on the message app which stupidly sends a message of a thumbs up without any confirmation. In his apology he offered to repay me for it, I told him not to bother as I was getting money and funding soon while he was bumming about the alps on a budget and I wasn't paying for fuel. For some reason he took offence to this and shouted at me saying I was being arrogant, sometimes I fail to grasp what goes on in that boys head when you try to do him a favour.

Driving to Austria we made it as far as Bregenz before we got turned around between roundabouts and the severe lack of signposts there are to be found around

Italian towns. After that it was pretty much smooth riding into Austria to a little place called Prutz near Landeck just West of Innsbruck.

On the way into Austria we stopped for lunch at the carpark of a gondola station, here I found an Ikea blanket and took a man of the mountains photo which rounded up the nudist adventures of this trip to Europe. This is also where I took the first few chunks out of a Giant watermelon that I'd bought out of a Eurospin for less than a Euro.

Campsite Tour

Arriving in Prutz we took a look around the campsite which was full of ancient, slow moving dutch people. Dan wasn't liking the look of these sketchy folk so drove us about 2 other campsites which looked really small and a bit limited so we drove back to Prutz and set up camp next to some other boaters from Loughborough Uni. First thing I did was begin folding my blanket to find the middle of it and used Dan's knife to cut a hole in it and thus was born my poncho which I quickly adopted as my new favourite bit of clothing. This was the first sign of my madness that Loughborough would bear witness to.

Getting Settled

Next we set up camp and attempted to tarp up ourselves some cover from the quickly approaching rain. Campbell's most prominent memory of his previous trip to Austria being that it rained the entire time. After a few shonky amateur attempts at this we finally found a configuration that worked with the tarp draped over our tents to give us a communal space between the two which we used as a kitchen/living room.

We set about making ourselves a meal we bought stuff for from Spar and I tried for first time aromat which is the ingredient used to give crisps and stuff beef flavouring. Really horrible for your insides but damn was it tasty. Loughborough then started to get more glimpses of the insane side of me that remained after the 3 days on my own. I did some funny decanting with plastic bottles and making funnels and vessels out of a drinks bottle for me to consume my 5L tub of wine.

Mad Man Melonhead (3)

After dinner we went over to join Loughborough uni for some drinks and this is where they got convinced I was mental. Carving out the watermelon I formed myself a helmet and also provided everyone with a tasty snack. Now the pyromaniac inside me from growing up in the country would show through. I filled the watermelon with my full bottle of Alcool and set it alight. Loughborough naturally panicked thinking who is this nutcase as I realised I had not planned how to put out the flames. I picked up some cardboard that was lying around and was going to use it to smother the flames... yeah that was a silly idea, I still maintain that the fire would have died before the cardboard went on fire if I sealed up the melon properly.

Instead I opted to put it out with a sheet of tinfoil which everyone also shouted at me in panic for but this wasn't my first time playing with fire and it worked.

I attempted to decant the alcool back into the bottle for later burning of the mouth and a juicy watermelon soothing aftertaste. This kind of worked it involved me messing about more with some bottles to make funnels that didn't really work and cutting notches in the watermelon to try and not have it run down the side. It didn't all work that well and I ended up spilling a fair amount on my joggies. Yes those maroon monstrosities made it on the trip.

After putting everything away from my first fire act I sat down with the lighter, in the past I'd set fire to pairs of jeans with deodorant and knew the rate of burning of the material would be enough for me to put it out should the alcool catch fire. Now I'd already taken everyone around me on a rollercoaster ride of worry for my own and their safety so I figured we might as well keep going. I set the alcool in the joggies on fire and everyone again panicked.

I patted it out quickly as this was me really just trying to prove to myself that I was right about the speed things would burn. After they were almost calmed from the first flame I lit it again and let it spread a little more. Then trying to pat it out my palm wasn't big enough to put out the entire flame. At this point even I panicked internally a little but I couldn't let that show and with some flustered rapid patting of my leg I did manage to get it out.

Not really registering the fact that we'd been drinking me and Dan jumped in his car to take it for a spin around the campsite(I don't drive, It was dark by this point and was raining) which was a fantastically stupid idea. Driving up to the gate of the campsite we got a bit too adventurous and turned out onto the road that ran along this side of the river, a quiet road but not empty, we did pass 1 car while out on the adventure. Dan decided to give me a driving test while out and I almost flawlessly performed a hill start and a simulated emergency stop with Dan hitting the bonnet. Luckily no one got hurt and we got back alright(gotta say I did a fairly good parking job too).

We then spent the next wee while playing games and drinking and getting to know one another before Loughborough decided to call it a night to get boating in the morning. Camo and Dan jumped off to bed as well but me and Campbell stayed up and got gibbled and phoned Becca(Campbells girlfriend) and our friends Mathias. Campbell spewing out the tent after drinking most of a bottle of Grappa Blanca.

Fruity Alpine Boating (4)

In the morning for some reason, probably just to be cruel to Campbell and toughen him up a bit we forced him to down the remainder of his Grappa Blanca and then got up and sorted out all our stuff, we had tried to get me a Buoyancy aid as it and a helmet were really the only 2 bits of kit there wasn't a spare of to get on the river and I was quite keen to get on. It's ok though as the night before we'd solved the helmet problem. With some Duct Tape we strapped the watermelon to my head once we got to the riverside.

To the joy of the other people boating with me we were not forced to ensure any more of my safety to the strength of Duct Tape and something remotely buoyant a rafting company turned up at the river and I gave them my details as an insurance to borrow a buoyancy aid from them and I had my full set of kit. The look of disbelief that I got from one of the rafting instructors as I bounded of telling him that I planned to use a watermelon as a helmet was the most intense I've ever seen.

At first getting on the river, I think some of my companions worried a little about the mentality/kayaking ability ratio I possessed (and I did a little too) but the further down we got the more people eased up and I made it down without even a capsize. I ran down to the rafting centre to hand in my borrowed BA and then all but me and a boy from Loughborough went on to do a 2nd river. I kind of wish I'd done the second river but at the same time I was happy to quit while I was ahead and return with only happy kayaking memories.

Top Notch Post River Chat

This was the first time I'd had experience of Camo's post river banter and I have to say it was top notch, I can't remember all that he did or do it justice in my writing but pretending to throw Campbell's nose in the river and delivering some fantastic one liners had me chuckling away. If Camo's cheeky banter wasn't enough then the moment one of the Loughborough accidentally flashed an Austrian couple walking by would have had you laughing. The guy gave an uncaring shrug while his wife gave an approving nod.

Another night of dinner and drinks, borrowing Loughborough's gas stove cause ours ran out of gas and the campsite didn't sell the right size of canister for what we had, and this would be my last evening in Austria. I set my phone up to charge in a little power box next to the tent and accidentally left the internet on so when I got up in the morning I had another day of my phone where I'd mucked up and had another day of phone use but also another charge on my account. So on a trip where I'd intended on using my phone maybe 2 out of the days I was abroad I'd managed to use it all 5 so far.

Before I was to be taken to start the return hitch I got to buckle in laughter once more at Camo as a dutch child next to us was crying and he was getting really infuriated with the noise. At one point both the parents had gone into the caravan and Camo turned round in rage to a baby alone in a highchair to which his brain instantly switched seeing humour in it all, "Oh a free baby!".

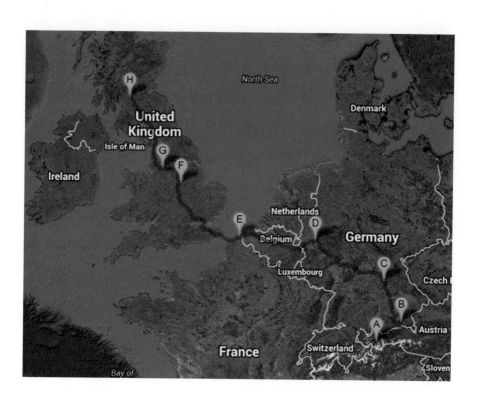

Homeward Bounds

Getting out of Austria

After some route planning and map reading using Dan's map I'd decided Landeck was the place for me to start hitching from. A lift off an outdoorsy type, a student trying to get his trailer road legal and an elderly man heading to Germany got me over the border and well on my way.

While travelling with the elderly guy I had some really good conversation he was a retired Doctor or Surgeon or something who was now working on a Patent for some technology he had researched was good company. He eventually dropped me off at a slip road just over the border in Germany.

Hermen the German, Jager Biller and the other characters.

My notes are a little sparse and my memory a little hazy on this bit of the journey and I can't really remember the chronology of events here but I will try to get it as close as I can.

I made some record time through Germany, my first lift spoke little English and got stopped by some kind of German authority figure. At the time I had no idea what was going on as they took my passport details and then drove off after a discussion with my driver. This was a really surreal tiem for me as I had no idea what was going on nothing was explained to me during the proceedings and my driver didn't have enough English to explain it to me afterwards.

Next lift was from a German man called Herman who I'd eventually got after much difficulty in trying to secure a lift. This is where I realised that the continent really was a different place for hitching and if you ask a German for help they are really helpful. After standing for ages at the exit of the service station I eventually switched tactics and began asking people around the place for a lift and eventually Hermen said he was going my way and gave me a lift, only a couple service stations up the road but enough to be helpful.

My next lift came from a Couple who had just returned from a cruise and were very caring and gave me some food and as I left a map of the German roads so I could easier communicate with people, here I was taught the phrase "Ich bin auf Reisen Schottland" which roughly translates to "I am going to Scotland" and these two things helped me at the next service station to get a lift from Biller.

Biller was a wonderful elderly German man who spoke little English but we tried our best to keep something similar to a conversation going in which I discovered he was a hunter in his spare time, a retired auditor of some sort and at one point while fiddling about with my wrecked glasses he turned off the motorway and took me into some small town where his opticians was and gave a woman 10 euro's to fix my glasses. This return journey is where I coined the phrase the kindness of strangers.

Another 2 lifts would see me all the way up to Koln from just South of Nuremburg. One of them a woman who made a point of telling me she didn't think I looked like a rapist and was a Doctor who had just got a new job at a Nuremburg Hospital and she managed to explain to me that the people who stopped me earlier were a force called the Zoll who do import control or something. The other from Nuremburg to Koln was a Turkish man who spoke 4 languages and I spent the journey learning German from him and teaching him some of the subtleties of English(he was an engineer and pronounced measurement "me sermont").

Cold dark Koln

By the time I got dropped off in Koln it was getting dark and the temperature drop was quite noticeable. I spent a good few hours walking about the service station asking for lifts getting a sarcastic "Haha If you can fit mate" from a man with a car containing 2 passengers and a tv(I'm pretty sure I could have fitted in around the tv).

I eventually spotted a car with a GB number plate and left him some comedy notes which I stuck in his door handle. I went into the café and asked if the Woman had met any other British people about recently and she told me he was probably a resident of the hotel across the other side of the motorway. Refusing/unable to pay into the hotel I looked for a spot in the trees to try and camp out, leaving the GB car another note. I couldn't find a decent place so I opted for the bench (another note).

While wrapped up in a sleeping bag with all my possessions tucked in at my feet a man who appeared homeless was wandering around raiding bins with a torch. He spoke quite good English and I offered him some food but he refused, so I wonder if he was too proud to take food from what must have appeared to him like a fellow hobo or if he wasn't raiding for food.

Eventually the cold got to me and I realised I wasn't getting any sleep so I went back out to try and get myself a lift again. I came across another GB number plate at the service station containing an elderly gentleman and a young boy but the driver seat was empty. A little later a Woman and her daughter began making their way toward the car from the toilet block and I approached them to ask if it was their car, I was told yes and asked where they were going; "Manchester".

Hungarian's (5) (6) (7)

I don't think I'd ever been so happy to hear the name of an English city before. After a quick consultation with the elderly gentlemen, who to this day I don't know if it was her husband with a huge age gap or her father, I was accepted into the car and proceeded to pass out between the 2 children. The obvious answer is her father but from the way they interacted it appeared more to me like a British married couple but maybe it's just a culture difference between here and Hungary where it turns out the family was from.

Their names were Patricia, Daniel, Ignac and Natalia. Natalia had been living in Britain for about 10 years now and worked in a shop. Daniel and Patricia were her children and Ignac... well he didn't speak much English. I was over the moon to have been taken in by this lovely family at half 3 in the morning at a service station in a foreign country. They really made me feel welcome and I got a lot more interaction with them than I did with the French family.

Turns out that Natalia had driven them all the way from Budapest without sleep and continued to do so until the Dunkirk ferry terminal. Even after the ferry where she must of only had, realistically, a half hour sleep, as we accidentally snuck into the truckers lounge, she drove us all the way to Nottingham.

The whole way arguing in Hungarian where the only word I could really pick out was koorva(I can't spell it) which I know from Polish is some kind of swear word. They have a really short fuse with one another which was amusing to me, especially when Natalia got lost at Dunkirk(an easy mistake to make having been in a car with Kian and Martin and attempting to navigate it before, this second time it made more sense to me and I think I get it now). I was less sympathetic when Daniel told me this isn't the first time she's done this and remembered she'd been travelling between Hungary and Britain for the past 10 years.

I got taught some Hungarian to use on Saba, a Hungarian friend of mine from Glasgow, which I still haven't got round to doing yet. She bought me food and drinks as we drove up through England and were just generally good people to travel with. When arriving at the border control at Dunkirk ferry terminal we were greeted by a moody English woman who proceeded to berate these nice people unnecessarily over some foster documents that she wanted Natalia to produce as it turned out Patricia was a foster child.

Getting past the beast that guarded the border to the ferry queue I had my first encounter with actual border control making an effort. While in the queue a man was walking round cars checking boots and spaces for hidden passengers and I assume illegal imports. I've come back and forth between Britain and Europe for 5 or 6 trips in recent years and this is the first time I've had any more than a passport check when travelling across the channel.

On the ferry I found Irony as I went for a wander in a Food Stop cafeteria where the shutter was down and the motto above read "For any time of Day". We'd also accidently spent the entire time sitting in the truckers lounge, I wondered why the ferry had been so much nicer than the last one.

Back on British Soil (8)

On the drive up through England we stopped at a shop and Natalia returned with some food and juice for me which I was really grateful for. I ran to a toilet in a neighbouring building and considered running back to charge my phone as it had died again since charging it on the ferry but I decided I didn't have enough time. I asked a woman in the car park if she had a USB charging slot in her car I could use for a few seconds to charge my phone and was given the response "No, and even if I did I wouldn't let you use it anyway." which brought me to the realisation that I was no longer in Europe and the kindness of strangers was significantly diminished.

As we drove North at one point I realised we were driving into Nottingham which is a bit further South East in England than the Manchester I was expecting. I panicked a little until I realised we were just dropping off Patricia with some relatives. And then Ignac took the wheel and drove us the final leg to Manchester. After having a lot of arguments about wrong turns and GPS in the car with Natalia, Ignac then took a wrong turn himself and Natalia smugly mocked him while you saw a look of defeat wave across his face before he quickly decided to stand his ground and shout back.

Robert Robertson, Paisley (9)

I finally left the Hungarians at Manchester Services where I finally got a Uk plug socket to charge my phone and had munch on some of the remains of the food I'd bought before leaving Austria and what Natalia had bought me. After making some calls and texts and probably doing a bit of facebooking I alternated for about an hour between approaching people for lifts and trying to hitch at the exit. I noticed a lorry from Ferguson transport driving past me at one point(A company from around Fort William who would most likely be heading past Glasgow) so I frantically attempted to write "I'm From Ft William" on my cardboard sign but didn't manage in time.

Eventually while walking around the car park I was offered a lift by a man called Robert Robertson from Paisley who was heading home and having some woman troubles via the phone at the time. He looked a little bit rough with some knife wounds and just in general but from talking with him it was clearly in his past and he turned out to be the old manager at the forge and now drove cars for a living between dealerships and such.

We had some brilliant chat ranging from spirituality and what it is to be human, through some politics and once again discussed probably the most asked question from my journey, "What's your view on Independence?" He was a good guy and in the end gave me a lift straight to my door.

31

Pen Chewing Reflections

1 Turns out I am human

Despite the passion I have for hitchhiking and doing ridiculous things, which anyone that knows me will probably already know of, getting myself to leave was actually one of the most difficult parts of the journey. My frequent involvement in ridiculous endeavours is not out of ignorance. I am, mostly, well aware of the oddities/improbabilities of the things I attempt do but I'll go along with them anyway and stay optimistic long after the average person because I enjoy the thrill of a new experience and have found a positive attitude is more helpful in achieving something than most realise. Other assets in these adventures are a largely unrecognisable comfort zone and sheer strength of will.

2 Coutt's Theory

The caverns that I got a tour of under the toll station in France were an oddly well decorated tunnel, which I assumed was for fire escape or something, for somewhere no one ever sees. Coutts had another theory though, what if this stocky little toll worker had for years been digging herself a series of caverns; looking back on it now no one else acknowledged their existence and the decorations were an off colour red.

3 Have faith in yourself

The whole time walking around Verona I knew where I was and I'd looked at maps and knew what way to go but because I was in a foreign country and it was dark and I was tired from the travel I didn't trust my judgement. Had I just trusted myself and my sense of direction, something I've always been pretty good with, then I would have gotten to the station in half the time.

3 Melon Draining

When I was draining the melon I don't know why I didn't think to just puncture a hole at the lowest point in the bottom so it would drain directly downward, when I realised this I was very disappointed in myself, even more so that it took several months of being back in Britain before it occurred to me.

4 BA.. Why not Helmet?

Another moment of stupidity I didn't catch till a lot later is why I didn't just ask the Feel Free guys for a helmet as well as a BA, if not for my own protection but so the others didn't feel so uneasy kayaking with me, part of me was probably just being stubborn and determined to kayak with this fruit.

5 Dunkirk

Basically as you're coming into Dunkirk from the East the port consists of several business units as well as the ferry terminal and the signage can be confusing in that it stops sign posting where the car ferry is and just starts pointing to all these numbered business units. Basically follow the signs for car ferry and nothing else it does disappear off the signs for a while.

6 Bordering on Bitch

Now I understand the need for border control and why the woman had to question Natalia on the Foster child, but Natalia had been told specifically by the Manchester foster agency that Patricia was 16 and could make her own decisions now so didn't think the documentation was necessary to have with her and she had not had it with her on any previous crossings apparently. Still these checks do need to be done. I don't have a problem with that, what I do have a problem with is the condescending and rude way the woman working for the border patrol handled the situation, there is no reason to be so cold to someone on suspicion alone. I came very close to stepping in and telling the woman how much of a cow she was being but I was worried it would cause more problems than it was worth for Natalia and co.

7 The Hungarian Edge

Knowing Saba here in Glasgow she comes across a little bit crazy, after meeting this family of Hungarians it became apparent that this is not just Saba it is a culture difference between British and Hungarians which, having seen in others, made Saba make a lot more sense to me.

8 British Mistrust

After the incident in the car park in England with a woman making a point to tell me that she would not offer me help with charging my phone even if she was able to(which I actually suspect she was given the kind of car she had) I was really taken aback. Having been in Europe for so long where people are just generally helpful and friendly to strangers by default It saddened me to realise that attitude doesn't get shipped across the channel. In general in comparison to our European counterparts Britain seems to be very mistrusting and fearful of strangers which is understandable to an extent given the media we are subjected to as a nation but it's not acceptable. It's a terrible blow to the sense of nationality and degrades what little form of society still remains here.

I don't know if this is just something from my experience but in general I have found this is most prominently the case in South/East England. It is much rarer that I have come across a Scot, Irish or Welsh person or someone from The West Coast / Northern England who had this extreme level of unhelpfulness.

9 Books and Their Covers

Spending those few hours chatting in the Car with Robert really opened my eyes to the level of judgements that we make about others. When I first got in the car with him I hadn't really gotten a good look at him and after a bit I started to be slightly wary of him as like I said he looked a bit rough and spoke with a Glasgow accent. A few more miles of driving and a lot of conversation I realised that I was being stupid and judging a book by its cover. Clearly yes in his younger day's he had come from a rough background but that was clearly all behind him and I can't help but think in a different scenario I wouldn't have given him the time of day.

This kind of upset me about myself and more so when I realised that I'm a very tolerant person, so if I do it then how much further must this kind of attitude go. It's a case of the old "to assume is to make an ass out of u and me" cliché and corny I know but it makes my point. Not only could my narrow-mindedness deny someone help which it wouldn't trouble me much to give but we could both benefit from the situation and I might be denying myself something worthwhile.

10 The Kindness of Others

After this journey and realising how kind everyone was to me during my travels I began thinking about the rest of my life and began to realise all the little things I appreciate in people and how much of my life is affected on this principle. Not just the kindness of strangers while I'm attempting to hitch hike but also the kindness of those around me on a day to day basis and all the little things we do for one another.

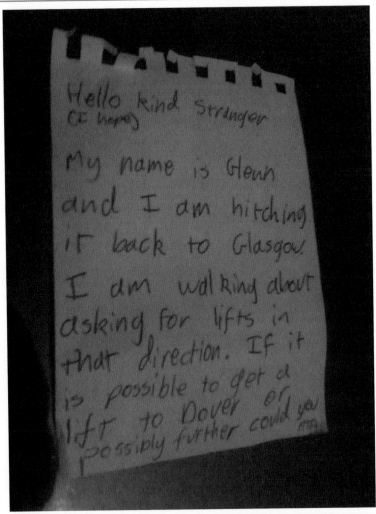

please wait around
for 6 or 10 minutes
(or if you can see
me, give me a shout)
I am wearing a blue
jumper and jeans. A lift
would be greatly
appreciated.

Cheers
Glenn McConnell
PS I have snacks

Hi Again,

I have now realised you are probably in the hotel. I have gone for a sleep. (can't afford the hotel so I am camping nearby) My number is 00778071436?. If you give this number a couple

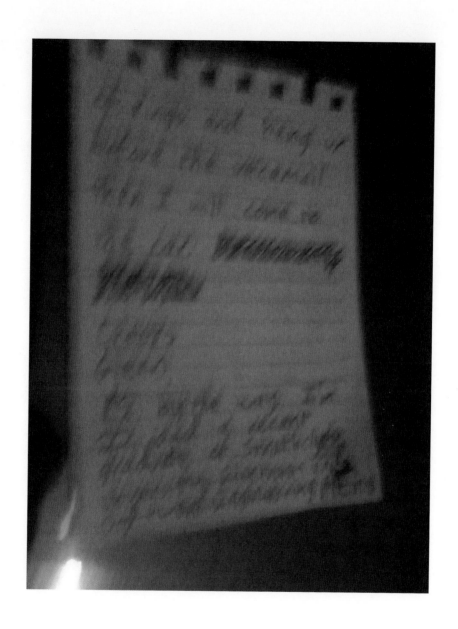

Hello Again,

Sorry for all the reading. If I've not left a 4th note, then you may have realised that's me on the bench. No where near as good for camping. Please wake me.

Cheers
Glenn

PTO.

More about me!

I kayak, curl, wakeboard, surf (badly) and snowboard. I am starting a Doctorate in September in Medical Devices.

PS Feel free to draw on my face/send me abusive texts if it turns out you hate hitchhikers, scots, sport participants or engineers.

I received no contact from them...

My thoughts

I can't help but think how much better a place the world would be if people thought about things like this a bit more often and caught themselves being prejudiced/passing up an opportunity to be helpful and thought about the times when the situation was the other way round and they had been shown kindness and understanding.

Next time you pass a hitcher or someone looks like they need a hand, think about the last time you asked someone for help either how good it felt when they said yes or how dejected you felt when they said no.

They might be scary looking or dishevelled but that's still someone's son/daughter standing there. Some of you will take the opposite view and think oh what do I gain from this or what about the minority who make the stereotype they do exist and I have encountered them, last week I nearly got punched for helping someone close a taxi door, but that doesn't dissuade me from it in the slightest.

To people like that, you gain nothing personally but humanity benefits, don't be so fucking selfish. Everybody needs help sometimes and you'd be surprised how much people can achieve when they get just a little bit of it. If the problems and hardships in this world are to be righted, then someone needs to put the effort in to improve things. Psst it's everyone. I know reading this I will come across to a lot of you as a hopeless hippy and to an extent I am but that doesn't stop me from being right.

I still haven't found out Preston's real name

18507941R00027

Printed in Poland
by Amazon Fulfillment
Poland Sp. z o.o., Wrocław